Dear James Beard

RECIPES AND REMINISCING
FROM YOUR FRIENDS
AND THE BEEF INDUSTRY COUNCIL

Copyright © 1984 by The Beef Industry Council,
National Live Stock and Meat Board, 444 North
Michigan Avenue, Chicago, Illinois 60611. All rights
reserved. Printed in the United States of America.
ISBN #0-88700-002-9
LIBRARY OF CONGRESS CATALOG CARD
NO. 84-070117
    Hu, Sandra Matsukawa and Day, Anne Leitch, eds.
    Dear James Beard, Recipes and Reminiscing from
    Your Friends and The Beef Industry Council

2229766

TABLE OF CONTENTS

James Beard is a national treasure. He has spent sixty-five years cooking, eating, observing and teaching Americans the many pleasures of food in this country, and no one has done it better. He has inspired new generations of chefs and food lovers to continue seeking the best of our country's generous food supply.

In these reminiscences and recipes from friends and associates, we hope to give a more intimate glimpse of this generous man and his world. We are proud to dedicate this book to Mr. Beard and trust he will forgive this bit of hero worship with his usual modest charm.

The Beef Industry Council

I love James Beard, and have known him as a good friend since the publication of our first _Mastering the Art of French Cooking_, when he was so kind. Here we were, Paul and Julia Child, who had been living abroad for 10 years and knew no one in the field, and Simone Beck, who was with us. He took us in, he introduced us around, he was all that a true colleague should be. I have always tried to follow his generous example in the profession, because it is James A. Beard who has set the tone, and he has done more for cooking in America than any one person in our history. This is a wonderful and most well-deserved tribute to our most noble American cook.

Mignons De Filet De Boeuf, Sautes Madere

1 to 1½ pounds (2 to 3 cups) trimmed tenderloin cut into 1½ to 2-inch pieces
¼ cup butter
1 tablespoon olive oil
2 tablespoons minced shallots or scallions
½ cup dry white wine or ⅓ cup dry white French vermouth
1½ cups excellent beef bouillon
2 tablespoons cornstarch dissolved in ¼ cup additional bouillon
Flavor additions as needed: pinch thyme, imported bay leaf, 2 tablespoons minced mushroom stems or 1 to 2 teaspoons mushroom duxelles or mirepoix vegetables (you may have some in your freezer), 1 teaspoon or so tomato paste or leftover fresh tomato sauce
⅓ cup dry (Sercial) Madeira
Salt and pepper

Dry beef on paper towels. Heat 2 tablespoons of the butter and the oil in a heavy frying pan large enough to hold all the beef easily in 1 layer. When butter foam has subsided, add beef. Let sizzle undisturbed 30 seconds, then toss it (swirling and shaking pan by its handle) several minutes until beef is nicely browned and, when pressed, has a very slight springiness—meaning it is rare. Transfer to a side dish and spoon all but 1 tablespoon fat from frying pan. Add shallots; sauté 1 minute. Add wine; reduce to almost nothing. Simmer bouillon in the pan, scraping into it all coagulated sauté juices. Taste and stir in flavor additions, simmering several minutes to incorporate. Remove from heat. When bubbling has ceased, blend in dissolved cornstarch mixture; return to heat, stirring, and simmer 2 minutes. Stir Madeira into sauce. Salt and pepper the sautéed beef; return to pan. Just before serving, bring sauce and beef to just below the simmer; fold beef and sauce together for several minutes, just to warm through. Fold remaining 2 tablespoons butter into sauce, turn beef out onto a hot platter and serve immediately with rice or noodles, a green vegetable, or baked or broiled tomatoes.

Makes 4 servings.

MASTERING THE ART OF French Cooking
BY JULIA CHILD
LOUISETTE BERTHOLLE
SIMONE BECK
Volume One

> **" . . . he has done more for cooking in America than any one person in our history. "**
> **Julia Child**

Julia Child first captured American attention and imagination in 1961, during a two-month national tour with Simone Beck to promote _Mastering the Art of French Cooking_. It led to the idea of a TV cooking series. The rest is history. Currently, Ms. Child is a columnist for Parade magazine, appears weekly on ABC's Good Morning America and has a new TV series, Dinner at Julia's.

I realize Jim Beard's incalculable effect on the ways we all eat. His influence on our national eating habits cannot yet be measured. He is an historical fact, gastronomically, like Pasteur and Freud and Picasso in other parts of our continuing existence. And the plain fact that I know him and love him is too astonishing to discuss.

The 15-Minute Meat Loaf (Plus 5)

This is a far cry from the dry meat loaves we once hoped might taste like a *pâté de campagne* rather than Sunday-in-jail, and it should be eaten soon, preferably with a big summer salad...

1½ pounds best procurable ground beef
3 tablespoons finely chopped onion
3 tablespoons chopped green pepper
1 can (8 ounces) tomato sauce
Generous teaspoon salt
½ teaspoon ground pepper

In the morning, for use that night or at least 8 hours later, combine all ingredients and mix well. Put into well-oiled baking dish in loaf form...that is, do not pack in, but make a small loaf in a large space. Chill. To serve, bake in preheated 450 degree oven on lowest shelf for exactly 10 minutes. Then place under lighted broiler for exactly 5 minutes. Remove at once, let stand for 5 minutes.

Makes 4 to 6 servings.

"He is an historical fact, gastronomically..."

M. F. K. Fisher

M.F.K. Fisher is best known for her gastronomical writings, beginning in 1937 with *Serve It Forth.* In the late 40's, she translated Brillat-Savarin's *The Physiology of Taste,* which has been republished. Ms. Fisher has been a housewife, mother and amateur cook. She has written novels, poetry, a screen play and for a few years she was a vineyardist in Switzerland.

My fondest memory of Mr. Beard is of his posing for a photograph in the pouring rain with Marion Cunningham in Big Sur on the ranch of Emile Norman, succeeding, if tenuously, to smile and not slide down the very steep slope on which the two were sitting. It was supposed to be a picnic and was anything but.

They were in Big Sur to attend a dinner I was giving for Mr. Beard at Ventana, an inn in Big Sur. The assembled guests included, amongst others, Mr. and Mrs. James Nassikas, Darrel Corti and Cecilia Chiang.

After the photo session was over the next morning, the group went up the precipitous driveway to

Emile Norman's house, right up in the clouds, where there was a roaring fire and Emile playing Bach on an organ modelled exactly after the one Bach composed on. I will never forget the look of peace on Mr. Beard's face in those surroundings. Nothing could have been more different from New York.

10

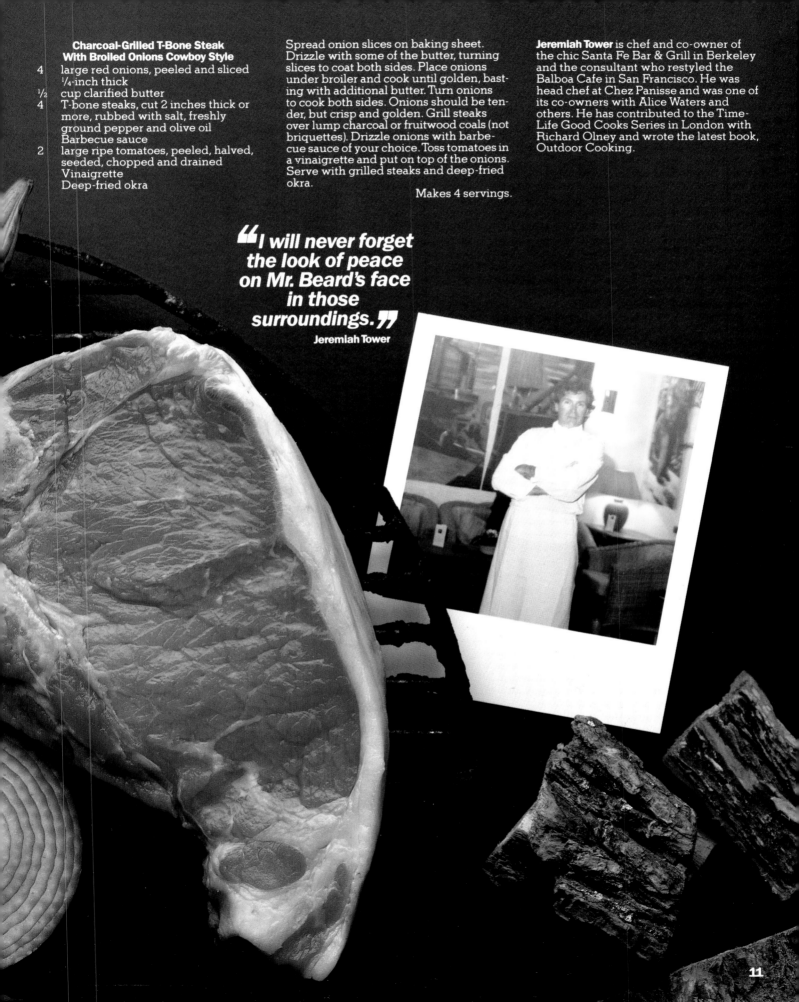

Charcoal-Grilled T-Bone Steak With Broiled Onions Cowboy Style

4	large red onions, peeled and sliced ¼-inch thick
½	cup clarified butter
4	T-bone steaks, cut 2 inches thick or more, rubbed with salt, freshly ground pepper and olive oil Barbecue sauce
2	large ripe tomatoes, peeled, halved, seeded, chopped and drained Vinaigrette Deep-fried okra

Spread onion slices on baking sheet. Drizzle with some of the butter, turning slices to coat both sides. Place onions under broiler and cook until golden, basting with additional butter. Turn onions to cook both sides. Onions should be tender, but crisp and golden. Grill steaks over lump charcoal or fruitwood coals (not briquettes). Drizzle onions with barbecue sauce of your choice. Toss tomatoes in a vinaigrette and put on top of the onions. Serve with grilled steaks and deep-fried okra.

Makes 4 servings.

Jeremiah Tower is chef and co-owner of the chic Santa Fe Bar & Grill in Berkeley and the consultant who restyled the Balboa Cafe in San Francisco. He was head chef at Chez Panisse and was one of its co-owners with Alice Waters and others. He has contributed to the Time-Life Good Cooks Series in London with Richard Olney and wrote the latest book, Outdoor Cooking.

> **❝I will never forget the look of peace on Mr. Beard's face in those surroundings.❞**
> Jeremiah Tower

*O*ne summer day about five years ago, James Beard and I were having lunch in a small truck stop cafe on the coast of Oregon. The woman who was all things to the operation, cook, dishwasher, waitress, stared at James with a puzzled, "I'm sure I've met you before" look. She studied him while cooking and at last the light dawned and she said to him in a shy, embarrassed way, "You're not?" He said, "I am..."

Beef Stew With A Top Crust

5	tablespoons fat
2	pounds beef chuck, cut in 2-inch squares
	Salt and pepper, to taste
1	quart boiling water
1	tablespoon lemon juice
1	tablespoon Worcestershire sauce
2	cloves garlic, sliced
1	large onion, peeled and sliced
2	bay leaves
	Pinch *each* allspice and ground cloves
1	tablespoon sugar
12	small boiling onions, peeled
5	carrots, peeled and cut into 1-inch pieces
2	tablespoons flour
	Pastry for 1, 9-inch pie crust (use lard for the fat)

Melt 3 tablespoons of the fat in heavy Dutch oven with a lid. When it is smoking hot, add beef; brown to a mahogany color, turning to cook all sides. Add salt and pepper while browning. While beef is sizzling pour in boiling water. Lower heat; add lemon juice, Worcestershire sauce, garlic, onion, bay leaves, allspice, cloves and sugar. Stir and let bubble a bit; taste and add salt and pepper, if more is needed. Cover; simmer for 1½ hours or until beef is tender. Add onions and carrots after the first hour. In small skillet melt remaining 2 tablespoons fat. Slowly stir in flour; cook and stir 2 to 3 minutes. Dip 1 cup beef liquid from stew; slowly add to flour mixture. Stir until thick and flour tastes cooked. Strain stew; place beef and vegetables in a casserole. Add 1 more cup of beef liquid to thickened sauce; stir until smooth. Pour over beef mixture in casserole. Roll out pastry 1 inch larger around than the casserole. Fit over casserole; crimp edges and cut 2 vents in top. Bake in 450 degree oven 15 minutes or until crust is golden and juices bubble.

Makes 6 to 8 servings.

Marion Cunningham has been teaching cooking classes for a dozen years. She is the West Coast Associate of James Beard and has assisted him in teaching classes all over the world. She revised the new edition of the *Fannie Farmer Cookbook* and has just completed the *Fannie Farmer Baking Book*, which will be published by Knopf in the fall of 1984.

> **❝...she said to him in a shy, embarrassed way, 'you're not?' He said, 'I am'❞**
>
> **Marion Cunningham**

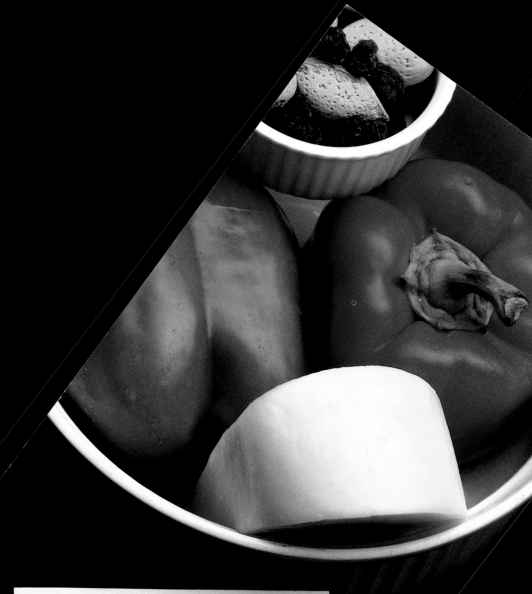

It is so difficult to find the words that can express the depth of my feelings for James Beard. For twenty years he has been a constant inspiration to me. Indeed, James Beard can truly be described by me as someone whom I regard with the same feelings that a son, who loves his own life and work, must have toward the father in his life who has been his model, tutor and inspirer. I cannot think of anything worthier of my respect and affection for this wonderful man.

Stuffed Monterey Jack

1	cup coarsely chopped onions
1	clove garlic, finely chopped
1	tablespoon olive oil
1¼	pounds lean ground beef
½	cup white wine
1	cup chicken stock
	Salt
	Crushed red pepper
	Ground cumin
½	cup diced red pepper
½	cup diced green pepper
½	cup seedless raisins
½	cup sliced almonds
1	cup cooked rice
1	tablespoon cornstarch
1½	pounds sliced Monterey Jack cheese
2	tablespoons bread crumbs

In heavy skillet simmer onions and garlic in hot oil until transparent. Add beef; brown over hot fire. Pour off excess fat. Deglaze pan with wine; add chicken stock and seasonings to taste. Cover; simmer 30 minutes. Stir in peppers, raisins, almonds and rice. Cook and stir 5 minutes or until almost all liquid has evaporated.

Blend cornstarch with 2 tablespoons water; pour over beef mixture. Stir in quickly with a wooden spatula; cool to almost room temperature. Line 3-quart soufflé dish with cheese, overlapping slices by ¼ inch. Chop and reserve trimmings. Pour in beef mixture; press lightly. Combine cheese trimmings with bread crumbs; sprinkle on top. Bake in 350 degree oven in water bath 45 minutes. Remove from oven; let stand at least 15 to 20 minutes. Unmold carefully onto preheated serving platter. Serve with boiled potatoes.

Makes 6 servings.

Swiss-born **Josef "Seppi" Renggli** is the culinary genius behind the scenes at the Four Seasons restaurant in New York City. The son of a construction worker, Renggli fell into the world of food when offered work in a restaurant at age 14. In two and a half years, he was cook, dishwasher, gardener and on his way to a career in food that would take him to the top.

66 . . . he goes
to a great deal
of trouble to seek out
the unusual. 99
Jacqueline Mallorca

16

James is one of those generous people who loves to surprise his dearest friends with lavish gifts of food at Christmas time, and he goes to a great deal of trouble to seek out the unusual. One year the surprise might be an enormous basket of fresh truffles flown in from France, another year it might be a splendid Kentucky ham, well aged and full of old-fashioned flavor. A few years ago he decided to send Chuck Williams some fresh quail eggs from a quail farm —they were very difficult to get at the time and he felt sure that Chuck would enjoy them. Well, the quail farm was happy to comply, but they got the size of the order a bit confused, and on December 24th, Chuck was the astonished recipient of ELEVEN HUNDRED fresh quail eggs. He spent the whole of Christmas day delivering baskets of quail eggs to all his friends like some kind of Easter bunny. James laughed for a week and Chuck still doesn't care for quail eggs much.

Classy Hamburgers

³/₄	pound freshly ground beef chuck
1	egg yolk
1	large shallot, finely chopped
1	pinch chopped fresh or dried thyme
	Salt and freshly ground pepper
1	teaspoon olive oil
1	teaspoon butter
¹/₂	cup red wine

Crumble beef into bowl; add yolk, shallot and thyme. (If using dried leaf thyme, use small pinch and crumble it well to release the oils.) Add salt and pepper to taste. Mix lightly but thoroughly with your hands; form into 2, 1-inch thick patties. Heat oil and butter in heavy skillet. Add patties; cook over medium-high heat for a total of 5 minutes. Turn them over 3 times after the first 2 minutes—the beef juices don't know which way to run, and stay in the beef this way. Transfer to warm plates, pouring off any accumulated fat. Deglaze pan with red wine over high heat, reducing it slightly. Strain over the meat and serve immediately. Good with sliced, pan-fried potatoes.

Makes 2 servings.

Jacqueline Mallorca, born in Scotland and educated in South Africa, is a free-lance food writer and illustrator. She writes the Williams-Sonoma catalog copy, is an editorial assistant to James Beard and is currently assisting Chef René Verdon with illustrations for a new cookery book. She combines a passion for good food with an equally compelling passion for horses.

The qualities I most prize in cooking are directness, honesty, generosity, imagination. All good cooks possess these to some degree. There is one individual, however, who through his published work, his conversation, his general presence embraces them so completely and expresses them so unequivocally that he is the living embodiment of—and his name shall enduringly stand for—the universally civilizing force of good food. Of all the marvelous things my career in food has brought me, one I shall forever be grateful for is to have known James Beard.

Il Tapolon Di Borgomanero
(Piedmontese Hashed Beef With Red Wine)

1/4	pound pancetta (Italian bacon) or salt pork, chopped very fine to a creamy consistency
4	tablespoons olive oil
4	tablespoons butter
2	tablespoons garlic, chopped very fine or mashed
2	pounds beef round, coarsely chopped
2	pounds Savoy cabbage, cut into thin strips
2	chopped bay leaves
3	whole cloves
1/2	teaspoon fennel seeds
1 1/2	cups Ghemme, Barbera or other stout, fruity red wine such as Zinfandel or Côtes du Rhone
	Salt
	Freshly ground pepper

Place pancetta, oil, butter and garlic in a large, lidded sauté pan. Sauté uncovered over medium-high heat until garlic becomes pale brown. Add beef, breaking it up with a fork. Brown well over high heat. Add cabbage, bay leaves, cloves and fennel. Continue cooking over high heat, stirring frequently, 2 or 3 minutes. Stir in wine, cover and reduce heat to medium-low. Cook 35 to 40 minutes, stirring occasionally. Season with salt and pepper. Serve with polenta or boiled rice.

Makes 6 to 8 servings.

From her forthcoming book to be published by Alfred A. Knopf in the fall of 1985.

Marcella Hazan, cooking teacher and cookbook author, first gained national renown with the publication of *The Classic Italian Cook Book* in 1973. Born in Cesenatico, a fishing village in Italy's foremost gastronomic region, she married Victor Hazan, an Italian-born American, and moved to New York in 1967.

"...he is the living embodiment of...the universally civilizing force of good food."

Marcella Hazan

About the time I opened the Stanford Court in 1972, James Beard re-entered my life. I had known him casually in Washington, D.C., in the sixties. Through James, I met his new-found friend, Marion Cunningham, who has since become his closest assistant at cooking schools, a world traveling companion and confidante. Marion was then struggling with the formative stages of a whole new career outlook... that of culinary author and cooking school teacher. Together we began annual cooking classes at the Stanford Court. Amongst the happiest moments I've ever witnessed was the day the phone rang in the tiny service kitchen where the cooking classes were being held. It was Judith Jones of Alfred Knopf offering Marion Cunningham the assignment to dramatically revise the Fanny Farmer Cookbook, which had not been done in over 30 years. James had recommended Marion. The euphoria, the tears of joy, the cries of delight were so heartwarming to us all. However, towering above the din and clatter I shall never forget the glint of fulfillment in this wonderful friend's eye... it told that a shared success is the best success of all.

Filet de Boeuf à la Ficelle
(Fillet of Beef on a String)

Beef:
3 quarts canned beef broth diluted with 2½ to 3½ quarts water (see Note)
  Bay leaf
2 tablespoons unsalted butter
2 tablespoons peanut oil
1 whole fillet of beef, trimmed (4 to 4½ pounds) and tied at 2-inch intervals, at room temperature
Garnish:
2 leeks (white part only)
2 carrots
2 ribs of celery
  Horseradish Sauce (recipe follows)

Place wire rack in casserole or stockpot 12 or 14 inches wide and at least 5 inches deep. Add 5½ quarts of the stock and bay leaf; bring to boil. Meanwhile, in large skillet, heat butter and oil. When foam subsides, add fillet; sauté over moderately high heat, turning occasionally, until browned on all sides, about 6 minutes. Remove from pan; loop around in a horse-shoe shape to fit in your pot. Tie ends together, leaving at least ½ inch slack so beef is not touching itself at any point. Leave a length of string at the end of the knot. Lower beef by the string into boiling stock. Add additional stock to cover beef, if needed. When stock begins to simmer, reduce heat; simmer gently 5 to 6 minutes per pound for rare beef. (Do not boil.) Meanwhile prepare garnish: Cut vegetables into julienne strips. Steam until just tender, about 2 minutes. When beef is done, let rest 10 minutes before carving. Cut ¼-inch slices; arrange on platter. Garnish with vegetables. Serve hot or room temperature, with Horseradish Sauce.
Makes 8 to 10 servings.

HORSERADISH SAUCE: Mix 1 cup sour cream, ¼ cup grated fresh horseradish and 1 tablespoon prepared horseradish to blend. Stir in 2 tablespoons cream; season with salt. Refrigerate.

James A. Nassikas, President, Managing Partner and Managing Director of the elegant Stanford Court on San Francisco's Nob Hill, is celebrating his 25th anniversary in the hotel industry. He looks back on nine consecutive Mobil 5-Star Awards, the Diplome de l'Excellence Europeenne, and the success of Fournou's Ovens, recipient of virtually every prestigious American dining award.

❝..I shall never forget the glint of fulfillment in this wonderful friend's eye...❞
James A. Nassikas

"...he is the perfect guest."
Cecilia Chiang

James has been a guest in my restaurant and in my home many times. And he is the perfect guest. I had expected one of his prominence to give cooking advice when in any kitchen, but he is curious about every ingredient and the way it is prepared. He is also enthusiastic and most complimentary of each dish. This, I think, is one reason James Beard is so widely respected.

Mandarin Salon De Cuisine

1½	pounds flank steak
1	heaping tablespoon cornstarch
1	egg
1	teaspoon baking soda
1	tablespoon water
2	tablespoons cottonseed oil
	Oil, for frying
2½	ounces rice sticks
1	cup bamboo shoots
12	pieces dried black mushrooms, soaked
½	yellow onion
12	string beans or other non-watery green vegetable
1	tablespoon wine
3	tablespoons oyster sauce
2	tablespoons soy sauce
1	teaspoon sugar
1	teaspoon salt
1	teaspoon sesame oil
1	tablespoon cornstarch/water solution

Trim flank steak; cut lengthwise in 2 or 3 strips, depending on the width of the steak. Shred against grain. Combine cornstarch, egg, soda, water and cottonseed oil to blend. Combine with beef; marinate for a couple of hours. Heat oil (for frying) in wok; fry rice sticks for a second or two. Drain with a strainer and crush gently; set aside on a platter. Shred bamboo shoots, black mushrooms, onion and beans. Heat oil in wok over high heat; add beef; stir-fry briefly while adding vegetables and wine. Stir-fry until vegetables are crisp-tender. Combine oyster sauce, soy sauce, sugar, salt, sesame oil and cornstarch/water mixture. Stir-fry to blend. Serve on a bed of fried rice sticks.
Makes 6 servings.

Cecilia Chiang, owner of the Mandarin restaurants in San Francisco and Beverly Hills, was born into a patrician lifestyle in Peking. She was inspired to appreciate fine cuisine by her mother, an excellent cook who supervised the family chefs. Ms. Chiang tells of her life in pre-revolution China in a memoir-cookbook, *The Mandarin Way.*

"*...your legion
of friends
around the world
share my
feelings.*"

Mary Lyons

24

Dear Jim. It was many years ago when we first met, but I was definitely introduced by our dear mutual and magnificent friend, Helen McCully, a few years later. Since then our friendship has become one which I personally cherish. For a thousand reasons — first, for your glorious spirit, second, for your depth of knowledge, a constant inspiration to me. The rest? Variations of the first two... I know your legion of friends around the world share my feelings. And, I'm delighted to say, so does the French government. Your medal of the Ordre du Mérite Agricole is only one of the many honors bestowed on you. I am proud to be included in your book and only hope my contribution makes you proud also.

Ragout Du Midi

2 tablespoons butter
2 tablespoons olive oil
3 pounds lean chuck, cut into 2-inch cubes
   Salt and pepper
2 tablespoons flour
1 clove garlic, chopped
½ cup chopped shallots
¾ cup beef broth
¾ cup French dry white wine
1 cup chopped carrots
¼ cup chopped celery
1 bouquet garni
2 medium zucchini, cut into ½-inch slices
3 medium tomatoes, peeled, seeded and chopped
½ pound small mushrooms, halved
¼ cup whole Nicoise olives
   Chopped parsley

In Dutch oven heat butter and olive oil. Add beef; brown on all sides. Sprinkle beef with salt, pepper and flour; toss with a fork until flour is absorbed. Add garlic and shallots; mix well. Stir in broth and wine; add carrots, celery and bouquet garni. Bring to boil; reduce heat. Cover; simmer 1½ hours. Add zucchini and tomatoes; cook 5 minutes. Add mushrooms and olives; cook 5 minutes longer. Garnish with chopped parsley.

Makes 6 servings.

Since 1970, **Mary Lyons** has been director of public relations for Food and Wines from France, information and promotion center based in New York City with headquarters in Paris. She is president of the New York Chapter of Les Dames d'Escoffier, member of several French wine brotherhoods and has been awarded the Ordre du Mérite Agricole by the French government.

For Jim Beard, a colleague and friend for more years than either of us cares to remember. Whenever, and wherever, we meet I look forward to his welcoming smile, a kiss, and with a twinkle in his eye, the latest gossip from the world of food. With affection.

New England Pot Roast

A delightfully spicy dish; the horseradish loses its pungency as it cooks.

3	tablespoons flour
1½	teaspoons salt
½	teaspoon freshly ground pepper
1	4-pound bottom round pot roast of beef
3	tablespoons vegetable oil
½	cup freshly grated horseradish or prepared, drained 4-ounce jar
1	cup whole cranberry sauce, fresh or canned
1	stick cinnamon, broken in half
4	whole cloves
1	cup beef broth
16	small white onions
1	bunch carrots, peeled and cut into 3-inch lengths
2	parsnips, peeled and cut into 3-inch lengths

Mix flour, salt and pepper; rub into all surfaces of beef. In heavy Dutch oven or casserole heat oil; add beef and brown on all sides over high heat. Pour off drippings into heavy skillet and reserve. Mix together horseradish, cranberry sauce, cinnamon, cloves and broth; add to Dutch oven. Bring mixture to boil, cover tightly and simmer gently 2 hours, or until beef is almost tender. Meanwhile brown onions in reserved drippings in skillet. Add carrots and parsnips; cook 4 minutes longer. With slotted spoon remove vegetables to Dutch oven. Add more beef broth if there has been evaporation. Cover; cook until vegetables are tender, about 25 minutes.

Makes 6 servings.

Jean D. Hewitt is food and equipment editor of Family Circle, the largest woman's service magazine in the world, with 7.5 million copies sold every three weeks. A former food reporter and critic of The New York Times, Ms. Hewitt also is the author of nine cookbooks, including The New York Times New Natural Foods Cookbook and the New York Times Heritage Cookbook.

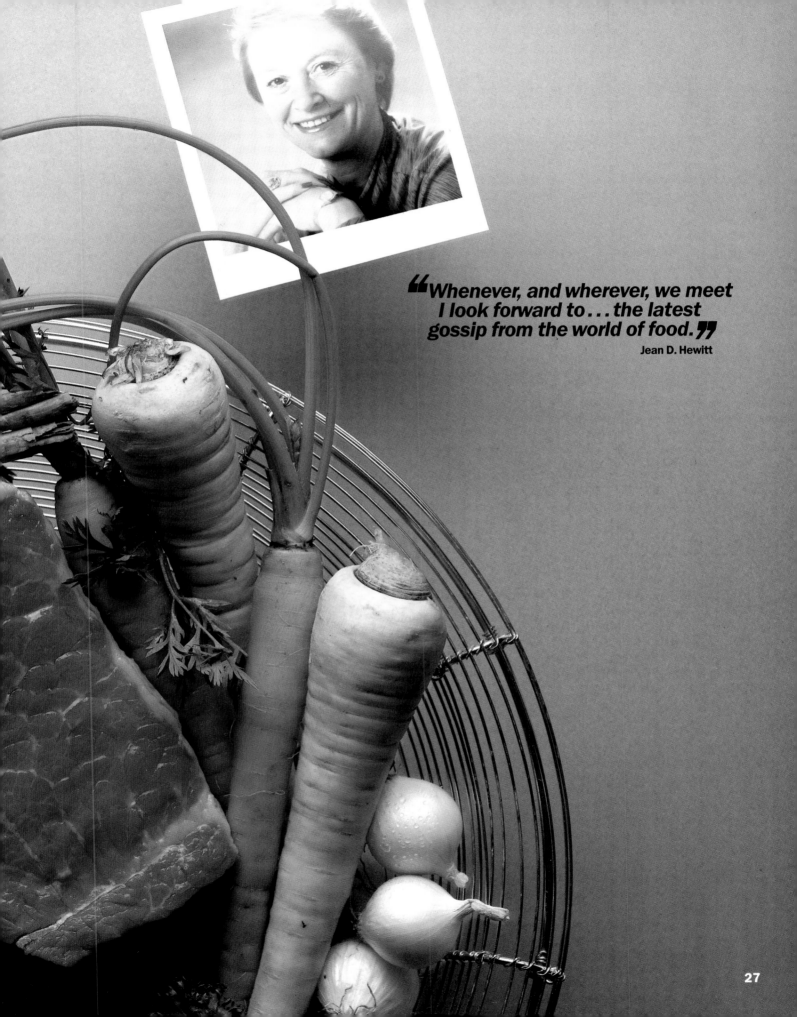

"Whenever, and wherever, we meet I look forward to ... the latest gossip from the world of food."

Jean D. Hewitt

James Beard is the most wonderful storyteller I know. He can say something informative and interesting about every little odd foodstuff you can imagine. I once cooked him a soup of immature heads of garlic that I thought he might not have had before because I had picked the garlic accidentally too soon from the garden. But when I served the soup, James said, "Oh, it's green garlic!" James has been at home for so long in the world of foods that my accidental invention was an old friend to him, with a name!

By sharing his captivating memories, James inspires us to seek out all sorts of foods we wouldn't even know about if not for his stories. Talking with James always confirms for me the richness and variation possible in American cooking.

Cold Grilled Fillet Of Beef With Rocket Salad

1	6 to 8-pound fillet of beef
2	medium yellow onions, peeled and sliced
2	bay leaves, crushed
10	to 12 black peppercorns, crushed
1	bottle red wine (Beaujolais or Chianti)
½	cup virgin olive oil
10	to 12 sprigs Italian parsley
	Salt and pepper

Completely trim beef of fat and connective tissue. Place in a large, wide dish. Put onions, bay and peppercorns around fillet, then add red wine, olive oil and parsley. Cover; marinate refrigerated for several hours or overnight, turning several times. Prepare a medium-hot wood charcoal fire. Remove fillet from marinade, rub with a little olive oil, salt and pepper. Fold thin tail of the fillet toward the center; tie securely to form a roll of even thickness. Put over hot coals when flames have just subsided. Cook about 25 minutes, turning 5 or 6 times for even cooking. The fillet is done when its internal temperature is 125 to 130 degrees or when it is firm yet springy when pressed lightly with a finger. Remove from fire; cut off strings. Cool completely. Carve into ⅜-inch slices on a slight diagonal. Serve with a rocket salad with vinaigrette and garlic mayonnaise.

Makes 8 servings.

Owner and chef **Alice Waters** opened Chez Panisse in 1971, offering regional foods prepared with innovation. Serving one five-course dinner each night, Ms. Waters refines the menus daily to utilize the best foodstuffs from a network of special sources. Ms. Waters wrote the *Chez Panisse Menu Cookbook,* published by Random House in 1982, and is now working on two more cookbooks.

"Talking with James always confirms for me the richness and variation possible in American cooking."
Alice Waters

"I'm delighted to recognize the "Dean of American Cookery." His encouragement over the years has been wonderful!"

Narsai David

Russian Beef Soup

½   pound lean ground beef
1   small onion, grated
     Salt and pepper
1   tablespoon flour
1   quart unflavored yogurt
1   quart beef or lamb broth
½   cup raw rice
½   cup drained garbanzos
2   cups chopped spinach leaves or
     sorrel and spinach
¼   cup chopped parsley
¼   cup chopped chives or scallions
¼   cup chopped dill

Combine beef, onion, salt and pepper
until smooth. Form into balls; set aside.
Beat flour into yogurt, then add broth.
Season with salt and pepper. Bring to
boil, stirring. When thickened slightly,
add meatballs and rice; simmer until
meatballs are cooked and rice is tender.
Stir in remaining ingredients. Taste and
correct seasoning.

                    Makes 6 servings.

Narsai David opened the popular Narsai's
Restaurant in North Berkeley in 1972.
The menu is classic French with a Medi-
terranean accent, reflecting his Assyrian
American heritage. Narsai's weekly
appearances on PBS TV's "Over Easy" and
his creative catering, such as Bill Graham's
1978 New Year's Bash for 6,000, have
given him celebrity status. He is working
on a cookbook series.

"A true kindred spirit!"
Loni Kuhn

James, my fondest memory of you is the first day of the first class in Seaside, many years ago. There was a lovely juicy chicken on the butcher block and right beside it, a very tempting gizzard, which I reached for to pop into my mouth. From the other side of the table shot out a huge hand, yours, and gleefully popped it into your own, grinning. A true kindred spirit! Before that marvelous day I never knew anyone but I loved gizzards. A revelation!

Lengua Chipotle
(Beef Tongue With Chipotle Peppers)

This recipe is from Sonora, Mexico, which is cattle country. It is very good served with a polenta-like cornmeal mush or black beans and is very good as filling for tacos or burritos.

Tongue:
1	beef tongue, about 4 pounds
2	onions, sliced
4	cloves garlic, chopped
2	bay leaves
	Parsley sprig

Sauce:
2	onions, chopped
4	cloves garlic
2	tablespoons salad oil
1	28-ounce can solid pack tomatoes
1	to 2 teaspoons cumin powder
	Salt and freshly ground pepper, to taste
½	can (6 to 7-ounce size) chipotle peppers

Simmer the tongue, onions, garlic, bay and parsley in salted water to cover, until tender, 3 to 4 hours. Lift tongue from broth; set aside to cool. Skin, trim and slice. Meanwhile, prepare sauce. Fry onions and garlic in oil until golden. Place in food processor with remaining ingredients; blend smooth. Place in heavy saucepan; add tongue slices and reheat gently, about 30 minutes.

Makes 12 to 16 servings.

Loni Kuhn grew up on a cattle ranch outside San Jose and learned to cook from the family's Italian housekeeper, as well as from Greek, Turkish, Lebanese and French friends. She studied with Marcella Hazan and James Beard. Ms. Kuhn has a cooking school in San Francisco. She is a magazine contributor and restaurant consultant. She has just introduced a new line of California foods.

I will always carry in my mind a picture of James Beard standing in front of his huge two-door refrigerator that is invariably crammed with bits of this and that, sticking his finger in some little container, sniffing, tasting, pondering—as though he were composing some gastronomic melody in his head —then pulling out what he wants and conjuring up some simple, delicious dish. A sense of true pitch always directs him to the right complementary seasonings, and I think he can almost hear when something is done as he pokes his head in the oven. I love his attitude that anything goes— or, at least, why not try it and find out—and I share his preference for meat that has some real chew and flavor to it. I remember once when he was on a salt-free diet he made an oxtail stew filled with earthy, sweet root vegetables and herbs and no one at the table even noticed that lack of salt, it was so flavorful.

I think James Beard would appreciate this simple but tasty flank steak that Evan and I often prepare for ourselves, as well as the dish we make from whatever is left over.

Gratin Of Steak Slices And Mushrooms

¾	pound mushrooms, chopped
3	fat garlic cloves, finely minced
6	shallots or scallions, finely chopped
¼	cup chopped Italian parsley
	Herbs: thyme, savory or tarragon, to taste
¾	cup fresh bread crumbs
	Salt
	Freshly ground pepper
¼	cup olive oil
8	thin, rare slices Broiled Flank Steak (use leftovers from recipe below)
2	tablespoons red wine

Mix mushrooms, garlic, shallots, parsley and herbs with ½ cup of the bread crumbs. Add salt and pepper to taste; mix in 2 tablespoons of the olive oil. Rub bottom of a shallow casserole with olive oil. Distribute half the mushroom-crumb filling on the bottom. Lay steak slices in single layer on top; season with salt, pepper and wine. Top beef with remaining filling and bread crumbs; drizzle with remaining olive oil. Bake, uncovered, in preheated 375 degree oven 25 minutes.

Makes 2 to 3 servings.

BROILED FLANK STEAK: Rub 1 flank steak with 1 tablespoon finely minced fresh ginger, 2 to 3 fat cloves garlic, chopped, and freshly ground pepper on both sides. Place in shallow dish with ¼ cup each soy sauce and dry sherry. Marinate 30 to 60 minutes, turning once. Broil steak 2 to 3 minutes on each side, brush with marinade, turn and broil 2 to 3 minutes more. Cut thin, diagonal slices. Use leftovers in Gratin of Steak recipe, above.

Judith Jones has been an editor at Knopf since 1957 and has worked with such writers as James Beard, Julia Child, Marcella and Victor Hazan and M.F.K. Fisher. She has co-authored with Evan Jones Knead It, Punch It, Bake It (1981) and The Book of Bread (1982) and recently collaborated with Angus Cameron on the L.L. Bean Game and Fish Cookbook (1983).

"I love his attitude that anything goes..."

Judith Jones

"He likes good fresh food simply prepared..."
Chuck Williams

In 1958 I established Williams-Sonoma on Sutter Street in San Francisco. The world had not yet heard from Julia Child and The Greats of the cooking establishment were few, and to me, legendary names as remote as the stars of Hollywood. Shortly after we had opened in June, one afternoon just before closing time, Virginia tiptoed into the back room and whispered, "I think James Beard just came in!" She was right. It _was_ James Beard and it was not only my shop but my life that he came into.

After all these years, when he is in these parts, even with his busy schedule, he manages to make it to my house for dinner several times a week.

Strangers tend to say, "Aren't you brave to cook for someone like that …I'd be terrified!" Nothing could be easier. He likes good fresh food simply prepared and that kind of fare is not only my specialty, it's the only kind I know.

Pot Roast Of Beef With Aceto Balsamico
(Vinegar Of Modena)

¼ cup olive oil
4 to 5 pound rump, chuck or bottom round of beef
1 onion, peeled and sliced
1 carrot, peeled and sliced
1 stalk celery, sliced
1 bay leaf
2 to 3 whole cloves
1 to 2 sprigs fresh thyme or ¼ teaspoon dried thyme
2 to 3 sprigs parsley
1 cup water
1 to 2 tablespoons aceto balsamico
Salt and freshly ground pepper

Heat oil in heavy pot with tight-fitting lid. Brown beef on all sides; remove and set aside. In same pot, sauté vegetables lightly until onions are transparent. Add bay leaf, cloves, thyme and parsley to vegetables. Place beef on top; add water and aceto balsamico. Cover tightly; lower heat and barely simmer 2 to 3 hours, until tender. After ¾ of the cooking time, add about 2 teaspoons salt and dash pepper. When done, turn off heat, let rest 5 minutes and remove beef to a warm platter. Skim fat from liquid; over high heat, reduce liquid to about one half (until thickened). Adjust seasoning; serve with meat, along with boiled potatoes or noodles.

Makes 8 to 10 servings.

Chuck Williams, founder, creative head and Chairman of the Board of Williams-Sonoma, began his cookware business in the wine country town of Sonoma, CA in 1956. In 1958 he moved the shop to San Francisco, where it remains today as the largest retailer of fine quality cookware in the country. Merchandise is purveyed through 15 retail stores and 30 million catalogs distributed quarterly.

"I doubt that there is an edible ingredient in the world that Jim wouldn't enjoy savoring..."

Maggie Gin

Having had the pleasure of cooking for James Beard on his visits to San Francisco in the past nine years, I am often asked, "What do you cook for a great cook and master of food?" My answer is as simple and easy as it is to cook for Jim. I doubt that there is an edible ingredient in the world that Jim wouldn't enjoy savoring, provided it is cooked correctly. I remember the first time Jim came for dinner, which was soon after the <u>Innards</u> cookbook I co-authored with Jana Allen came out. Jim enjoyed this book and wrote about it in his column. There was one dish Jim requested when he came for dinner... Pig's Ear Salad... composed of julienne cut pig's ear, carrots, cucumbers, scallions, sesame seeds, tossed with a sweet and sour dressing. He loved it!

5-Spice Beef and Chinese Cabbage

2	pounds beef stew, cut in 1-inch cubes
3	tablespoons peanut oil
2	thin slices fresh ginger root, minced
½	teaspoon 5-spice powder
2	tablespoons soy sauce
1	tablespoon oyster sauce
2	tablespoons sherry
1	teaspoon sugar
2	green onions, cut in 2-inch lengths
2	sprigs Chinese parsley, chopped
3	cups stock or water
1½	pounds Chinese cabbage

In wok, Dutch oven or large, heavy pot, brown beef in oil about 5 minutes. Add remaining ingredients except cabbage. Bring to gentle boil; lower heat. Cover; simmer 1½ hours or until beef is tender. Meanwhile, cut cabbage in 2-inch chunks; put in separate pot with ½ cup water. Cover; steam 10 minutes or until cooked. Drain; put on a platter and top with cooked stew with some of its juices.

Makes 6 servings.
NOTE: This stew is also delicious served on freshly cooked noodles.

Maggie Gin's culinary heritage is a unique combination of Chinese and the American West. She was born in Tucson, where her parents settled after leaving Canton. Formerly a sportswear designer, Ms. Gin also has been a restaurateur, cooking teacher, author of six cookbooks and is now engaged in continuing product development for her line of bottled sauces and salad dressings.

The very first time I met James Beard I was brought to his house to be interviewed about an editorial project. Nervously I showed off, trying to put myself in a good light. Disastrously, I delivered myself of a piece of misinformation. James rose to his not inconsiderable height and thundered off in a terrifying rage, saying, "I can't work with that woman." A few moments later, he relented, explaining that it had been a tiring day. Since then we have worked together many times; but I have been very careful that I really knew what I was saying when I spoke. James has been the most extraordinary education as well as friend. His sense of the audience —what it wants to hear and know, its taste—and how to make himself really useful and available to it is extraordinary. His sense of the history of food and its essential relationship to general history and mores is vast. We have taught together, complained together, eaten together and laughed together. A better and more interesting friend is impossible to imagine.

Short Ribs

3	tablespoons vegetable oil
¾	cup diced onion
½	teaspoon minced garlic
4	short ribs of beef (2½ pounds total), each 4½ x 2½ inches
⅔	cup flour mixed with 1 teaspoon kosher salt and ¼ teaspoon freshly ground pepper
¼	cup cognac
⅔	cup dry red wine
1	cup beef stock
¼	cup fresh orange juice
3	(2-inch) strips orange zest
½	cup Nicoise olives
¼	cup chopped parsley

Heat oil in Dutch oven; sauté onions 3 to 5 minutes. Add garlic; continue to sauté until onions are translucent. When cooked, remove from pan with slotted spoon, leaving fat in pan. Set aside. Dredge ribs with seasoned flour mixture. Sear in hot fat to brown all sides. Remove; reserve with onions. Pour fat out of pan. Deglaze with cognac, scraping bottom with a wooden spoon and cooking rapidly. Add wine and stock; let mixture boil rapidly 2 minutes. Return short ribs and onions to pan. Add orange juice and zest. Lower heat to a gentle simmer. Cover; cook 1 hour. Add olives. Cover; cook until beef is tender, about 30 minutes longer. Remove beef to a platter. Sprinkle with parsley. Skim fat from sauce. Serve with the sauce and a creamy polenta.

Makes 4 servings.

NOTE: If the sauce is too weak, remove olives, reduce sauce by rapidly boiling. Return olives to the sauce. Correct with lemon juice, salt, pepper and glace de viande.

Barbara Kafka is president of Barbara Kafka Associates, a food and restaurant consulting firm. She authored American Food and California Wine, edited The Four Seasons Cookbook and was executive editor of The Cook's Catalogue. Ms. Kafka developed the magazine, Cooking, for Cuisinart and was consultant to Simac and Robot Coupe. She is the inventor of the BK 1000™ Power Whisk.

"His sense of the history of food and its essential relationship to general history and mores is vast."
Barbara Kafka

*D*ear Jim. I wonder if he has any idea how many unlikely careers he has launched, how many cooks he has inspired. There isn't another soul in this business who has been mentor and treasured friend to so many. The special kind of ideas and insights one finds in his books have long been my pilot light—and could have been conceived only by him. I simply love the man. Like a few other giants in their fields, Jim is exceptionally well-suited to the pleasures of his work.

I love to eat with him in a restaurant—it's almost like a Broadway show, waiters and proprietors dancing around his table with delicacies not offered common mortals, which he shares with gusto along with his great wit and style.

"The special kind of ideas and insights one finds in his books have long been my pilot light. "
Maggie Waldron

Chow

3/4 cup soy sauce
Juice of 2 large lemons
2 tablespoons grated fresh ginger
6 tablespoons Dijon-style mustard
6 tablespoons packed brown sugar
4 to 6 shallots, finely chopped
2 tablespoons finely chopped Jalapeño or Serrano peppers
2 racks beef spareribs (about 3½ pounds *each*)
Chinese greens and vegetables (cabbage, spinach, sugar peas, bean sprouts, whatever)
Chinese parsley

Mix soy sauce, lemon juice, ginger, mustard, sugar, onion and peppers. Whisk to blend thoroughly; reserve half for dressing. Pour remaining half over ribs in shallow dishes. Cover and refrigerate 1 to 4 hours, turning once or twice. Drain ribs, reserving marinade. Grill over hot coals of mesquite until crisp and browned on outside, but still pink inside, brushing with marinade. Serve ribs with greens and vegetables; sprinkle with lots of Chinese parsley. Dress with reserved soy mixture.

Makes 6 servings.

Maggie Waldron is a Senior Vice President and Director of the Ketchum Food Center in San Francisco and New York, offering clients a wide range of capabilities including test kitchens on both coasts. Before joining Ketchum, Ms. Waldron ran her own consulting business. She was an associate editor of McCall's, a director of television production and has authored several books.

42

The first time I saw James Beard was in a Manhattan restaurant in 1968. I spent my entire lunch watching him eat a mixed grill with joy and gusto. What impressed me, though, was that he ate so beautifully. When he had finished, there were two little white lamb bones sitting on the whitest bone china plate. We finally met in 1973. I cooked for him and some friends while he sat on a stool watching and giving his critique. I was extremely nervous and when I asked someone to wash a pot for me, he said: "A good cook cleans up after himself." I have tried to do that ever since.

I have watched Jim Beard over the years at his classes, I have dined with him, sought his advice, heeded his suggestions, and been touched by his generosity. But more, I have been amazed by his zest for living and his incredible knowledge of all things culinary.

Steak Tartare

½ pound sirloin, trimmed of all fat and cut into ¼-inch thick slices
2 tablespoons chopped shallots
2 tablespoons chopped parsley
2 tablespoons capers
2 to 3 tablespoons fresh mayonnaise (made with ½ olive oil and ½ vegetable oil)
2 tablespoons cold catsup
Salt (preferably kosher) and freshly ground pepper

Using a sharp chopping knife, slice steak into strips lengthwise, then crosswise. Chop strips again with one or two knives for a couple of minutes. Mix the beef with shallots, parsley and capers and continue to chop until the mixture resembles chopped beef, but is not as fine or mushy. Place mixture into a chilled bowl. Add mayonnaise and catsup; season with salt and pepper. Serve on thin slices of black bread with a small amount of black or golden caviar, or as a supper course, with crisp fresh lettuce, such as Bibb, salad bowl, or radicchio, a wedge of lemon, hot toast and sweet butter.

Serves 4 to 5 as an appetizer, or 2 as a meal.

Christopher Idone co-founded the New York-based catering company Glorious Food in 1971. He is now director of Glorious Food 2, a restaurant and food development company, and is the author of *Glorious Food*, published by Stewart, Tabori & Chang. He gives cooking classes and lectures and contributes articles to Gentlemen's Quarterly and Art & Antiques. He is currently completing another book.

THANK YOU'S

Beef Industry Council	*Publisher*

Ketchum Food Center
  Maggie Waldron
  Dorothy Nicholson
	Food Design

Bruce Wolfe	*Concept Design*
Karla Jacobs	*Creative Coordinator*
Sandra Matsukawa Hu	*Editor*
Terry Heffernan/Light Language	*Food Photography*
Frye & Smith	*Printer*

Individual Photo Credits

pp. 4, 6, 12, 19	Dan Wynn, New York
p. 8	Annie Liebovitz, New York
p. 14	Brigitte LaCombe
p. 21	Lans Christensen
p. 29	Bob Day
p. 30	Jeff Weissman
p. 36	©Metropolitan Home Magazine
p. 39	Karla Jacobs, San Francisco
p. 42	Fred Lyon, San Francisco
p. 45	Rico Puhlmann

Recipe Credits

p. 6	From *Julia Child's Kitchen* ©1975 Alfred A. Knopf, Inc.
p. 19	From the forthcoming book by Marcella Hazan to be published by Alfred A. Knopf, Inc., in the fall of 1985
p. 23	From *The Mandarin Way* ©1980 California Living Books